Aunt Lydia's Designs

American Thread Company

Alpha Editions

This edition published in 2022

ISBN: 9789356086661

Design and Setting By

Alpha Editions

www.alphaedis.com

Email - info@alphaedis.com

As per information held with us this book is in Public Domain.

This book is a reproduction of an important historical work. Alpha Editions uses the best technology to reproduce historical work in the same manner it was first published to preserve its original nature. Any marks or number seen are left intentionally to preserve

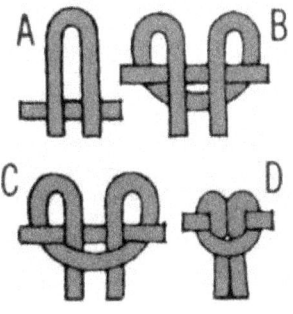

FIG. 1

FIG. 2

FIG. 3

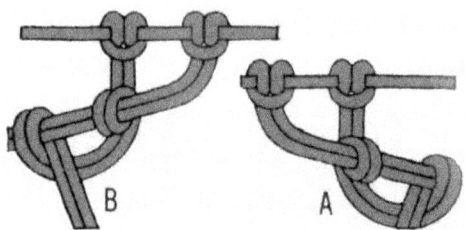

FIG. 4

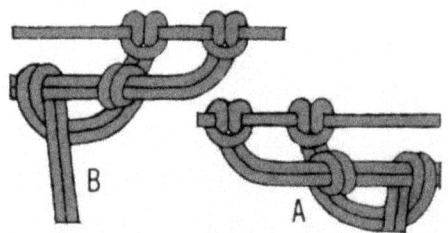

FIG. 5

MACRAME General Instructions

EQUIPMENT: T-pins. Scissors. Tape measure or ruler. Knotting board (brown paper marked off in one inch squares for gauge. Place over knotting board of Celotex, cork, or padded cardboard). Rubber bands for bobbins (wind lengths overhand, secure with rubber band and release as needed). 1-yarn needle.

KNOTTING: 1. Keep the foundation yarn secure and in place by using T-pins in the overhand knot at either end. 2. Keep leader taut and straight on an angle or parallel to the foundation yarn. 3. Tie knots tightly to cover leader. 4. Secure with pins to keep accurate measurement. (Use the one inch squares as a gauge.)

Learn all knots on sample piece before beginning, making sure to acquire the right tension. This will enable you to identify the knots.

Five knots are used in this booklet. They are basically the same differing mainly in direction. 1. Reversed Double Half Hitch (R D H H) as shown in figure #1, used for mounting lengths onto foundation yarn. Fold length in half, tuck looped end over foundation yarn and pull toward you, tuck loose ends into loop and tighten. 2. Overhand Knot (O H K) as shown in figure #2. Hold length in left hand, with right hand bring it up and over towards the left through loop formed, tighten. 3. Vertical Half Hitch (V H H) as shown in figure #3. Hold one length in left hand, with right hand bring next length around and between the two lengths (counts as one knot). Bring left length around right and between the two lengths. Continue for the number of knots indicated. 4. Diagonal Double Half Hitch (D D H H) as shown in figure #4. Working from left to right, the leader (length on which the knots are tied) is held in the right hand. Each length is knotted onto it in the same manner as the first knot of the V H H two times. The leader is held taut and on a downward angle. Working from right to left the leader is held in the left hand. 5. Horizontal Bar or Horizontal Double Half Hitch (H B or H D H H) as shown in figure #5. Holding the leader taut and parallel to the foundation yarn work as D D H H.

Asterisk...*. This indicates that the directions immediately following are to be repeated the given number of times in addition to the ones already given. Thus "repeat from * 3 times" means 4 patterns in all.

Belt

Material Required:

AMERICAN THREAD

"Aunt Lydia's" Heavy Rug Yarn.

2—70 Yd. Skeins color **A**.

1 Crochet Hook Size H or any size hook which will result in stitch gauge below.

Gauge: 1 pattern = 1 inch.

Suggested Color Scheme: A—Lilac.

Measurements: Waist: Fits All Sizes. Width: Approx. 4¼ inches.

With A and Size H hook, ch 15.

ROW 1: Dc in 4th st from hook, dc in next 2 sts, working over side of last 3 sts, insert hook in space between ch at beg and first dc, work a sc pulling loops to width of the 3 dc, * skip next st of ch, dc in next 3 sts, insert hook in space between these 3 sts and sts of previous group, work a sc, repeat from * once, dc in next st, turn.

ROW 2: Ch 3, skip 1 st, dc in next 3 dc, taking care not to work over the loop of sc of row below, insert hook in space between ch at beg and first dc, work a sc over the 3 dc just made, * skip next st, dc in next 3 dc, work a sc over side of these 3 sts, repeat from * once, dc in next st. Repeat Row 2 for waist measurement minus 2 inches.

FINISHING:

Working across long edge; sc, sl st, sc, sl st over side of last dc; sc, sl st over side of each row to next corner, sc, sl st in corner, * sc, sl st in same space, repeat from * once, * sc in next st, st in next st, repeat from last * 4 times, sc in next st. Continue around in same manner working next corners same as 2nd corner, end to correspond, fasten off.

TASSEL: (Make 2)

Wind yarn 30 times around a 5 inch cardboard. Tie one end; cut other end. Tie again 1 inch below first tying.

TIE:

Work a ch 36 inches long or length desired, sl st in each st of ch, fasten off. Lace through 4 front spaces of belt and attach tassels.

Instruction on page 8

HAIRPIN LACE AND KNITTED PONCHO

Size: Small

Materials Required:

AMERICAN THREAD

"Aunt Lydia's" Heavy Rug Yarn.

7—70 Yd. Skeins Color **A**.

2—70 Yd. Skeins Color **B**.

1—Pr. Jumper Knitting Needles No. 8 and 1 Crochet Hook Size H or any size needles and hooks which will result in stitch gauge below.

1—3 inch Hairpin Staple.

Gauge: On Knitting Needles:

7 sts = 2 inches; 7 rows = 1 inch.

Suggested Color Scheme:

A—Peacock; B—Bongo.

Directions are given for Small size.

Measurements:

Shoulder-arm length 19 inches.

HAIRPIN LACE:

With crochet hook make a loop, drop loop. Remove bar from staple, place dropped loop on left prong with yarn to front of staple, replace bar. Working with bar at bottom and curve at top, pass yarn over right prong to back of staple keeping the beg of loop at center. Insert hook through loop and pull yarn through, yarn over and pull through loop, * drop loop from hook, turn staple toward you to the left, pass yarn over right prong to the back, pick up dropped loop, pull loop tight and keep in center, insert hook under top part of loop on left prong, pull yarn through (2 loops on hook), yarn over and pull through both loops, repeat from * for desired length.

FIRST SECTION:

With B, and 3 inch Hairpin Staple, work a strip of hairpin lace having 123 loops on each side of staple, fasten off. Remove bar. Using Size 8 knitting needles working along 1 edge of hairpin lace and keeping 1 twist in each loop across, attach A in first loop, pull yarn through same loop, * insert needle in next loop, pull yarn through, repeat from * 58 times (60 sts), place a marker, insert needle through next 3 loops, pull yarn through all 3 loops (center st), place a marker, * insert needle in next loop, pull yarn through, repeat from * across rem 59 loops (121 sts on needle).

ROWS 1-3: (Garter st), K each row, slipping markers.

ROW 4: K 2 tog, K across to within 2 sts of first marker, K 2 tog, slip marker, K 1, sl marker, K 2 tog, K to within last 2 sts, K 2 tog.

ROWS 5-84: Repeat the last 4 rows 20 times.—37 sts remain.

ROW 85: K 1, * YO, K 2 tog, repeat from * across row (beading).

ROW 86: K across row counting the YO as a st.

ROW 87: Bind off. With A and size 8 needles, working on upper opposite side of hairpin lace, keeping 1 twist in each loop, pull up a loop in each loop of hairpin lace.—123 sts.

ROW 1: K—123 sts.

ROW 2: Inc in first st, K 59, inc in next st, K 1, inc in next st, K 59, inc in last st.—127 sts. (To Inc: K into the front and back of same st).

ROWS 3-5: K.

ROW 6: Bind off.

SECOND SECTION:

Work same as first section.

FINISHING:

With matching colors weave center seams tog matching rows.

COLLAR:

With B and 3 inch Hairpin Staple, work a strip of hairpin lace having 74 loops on each side of staple. Fasten off. With Size H hook, attach B in first loop, keeping 1 twist in each loop, work 1 sc in each loop along one edge. Fasten off. Having right side of poncho and collar facing, sew sc edge of collar to poncho, matching edges at center front seam.

CORD:

Take 2 strands of A, each 2½ yds. long, twist tightly, fold in half and let twist itself. Knot each end.

TASSELS: (Make 2)

Wind B, 25 times around a 4½ inch cardboard. Tie one end, cut other end, then tie again about 1 inch below first tying. Trim tassels. Lace cord through beading and attach a tassel to each end.

LAZY DAISY CLUSTER PILLOW

Materials Required:

AMERICAN THREAD

"Aunt Lydia's" Heavy Rug Yarn.

5—70 Yd. skeins color **A**.

1—70 Yd. skein each of colors **B**, **C**, and **D**.

1 Crochet Hook Size I or any size hook which will result in stitch gauge below.

Gauge:

3 rows = 1 inch;

5 sts = 2 inches.

Kapok or shredded foam rubber for filling.

Suggested Color Scheme:

A—Red; **B**—White; **C**—Yellow and **D**—Fern Green.

Size: Approx. 15 x 15 inches

FIRST SIDE:

With **A** and Size I hook, ch 38. **ROW 1:** Sc in 2nd st from hook and in each rem st of ch. Ch 1 to turn all rows.—37 sts. **ROWS 2-45:** Sc in each sc. Fasten off.—15 inches.

SECOND SIDE:

Work same as first side.

EMBROIDERY:

With **B** embroider daisies in lazy daisy st. With **C** work French knot in center (twice around needle). With **D** embroider leaves in lazy daisy st; calyx and stems in satin st. With **C** embroider large cluster in French knots. Cluster should be 4½ inches long, 3½ inches at widest point tapering to ½ inch at top as illustrated. Embroider small cluster in same manner 3½ inches long, 2½ inches at widest point tapering to ¾ inch at top.

FINISHING:

Place sections tog wrong sides facing. Sew 3 edges tog, matching rows. Fill with kapok or shredded foam rubber. Sew rem side.

MULTI-COLOR CHOKER & BELT
Instruction on page 14

MULTI-COLOR CHOKER & BELT

Materials Required:

AMERICAN THREAD

"Aunt Lydia's" Heavy Rug Yarn.

1—70 Yd. Skein each of **A**, **B**, **C**, **D**, and **E**.

1—1½ inch plastic ring for center of belt.

1—1 inch plastic ring for center of choker.

1—Yarn needle.

Measurements For Choker:

1¾ inches wide, 11 inches long.

Measurements For Belt:

3 inches wide, 24 inches long.

Color Scheme: **A**—Watermelon. **B**—Lilac. **C**—Orange. **D**—Spring Green and **E**—Turquoise Icing.

CHOKER

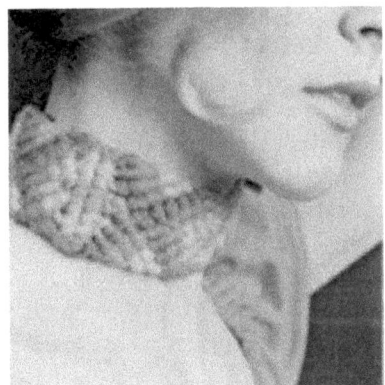

Cut four 1½ yd. lengths each of **A, E, D, C**. Cut four 2½ yd. lengths of **B**. Anchor to 1 inch ring, using the **RDHH**, in this manner: * (one half of the ring) 1 **B**, 1 **A**, 1 **C**, 1 **D**, 2 **E**, 1 **D**, 1 **C**, 1 **A**, and 1 **B**. Repeat from * on other half of ring. (**NOTE:** All yarns are worked two strands to a length). One half of choker is worked, then the other. * Starting with **E**, cross them over one another and work in opposite directions in **DDHH** having last knot 1 inch below ring. Repeat with all colors leaving lengths used as leaders untied until **B** is in the center. With **B** tie **3 VHH**. Pick up **E** and work each to center in **DDHH**. Repeat with all colors, leaving lengths used as leaders untied until **B** is on the outside. With **E** tie **3 VHH** *. Using outside **B** on left, work to right forming a **HB**. Do not tie **B** onto **B**. Using outside **B** on the right work to the left forming a **HB**. Repeat between *'s once, having the last knot of the **DDHH** 1 inch below last **HB**. Using outside

B on the left, work to the right forming a **HB**. With this length and the right outside length of **B** tie **14 VHH**. This will be sewn into place forming a loop. With a yarn needle or crochet hook weave in the ends on the back side for at least ½ inch. Trim. **BRAID:** Cut 6 one yard lengths of **B**. Tie all lengths together with an **OHK** two inches from beginning. Braid, using 2 strands of yarn as one, for twenty inches. Tie an **OHK**. Cut lengths 2 inches below **OHK**. Insert braid through loops for fastening.

BELT

Cut eight 6 yd lengths of **B**, four 5½ yd lengths of **A**, eight 5 yd lengths of **D**, four 5 yd lengths of **C** and six 4½ yd lengths of **E**. Anchor to 1½ inch ring in the following sequence using **RDHH**; * 2 **B**, 1 **A**, 1 **C**, 2 **D**, 3 **E**, 2 **D**, 1 **C**, 1 **A**, and 2 **B** *. Repeat between *'s for other half of ring. (**NOTE:** All yarns are worked 2 strands to a length except **E** which uses 3 strands as one). * Take **E**, cross strands over each other and carry to outside in **DDHH** so that the last knot is approximately 1 inch from the ring. (**FIRST ROW SHAPING ONLY**) Repeat with all colors, leaving lengths used as leaders untied, until **B** remains in the center. Pick up **E** and work to center in **DDHH**. Repeat with all colors, leaving lengths used as leaders untied until **B** is on the outside. With **E** tie **6 VHH**, with **D** tie **5 VHH**. Using outside **B** on the left, work to the right forming a **HB**. Using outside **B** on the right, work to the left forming a **HB** *. Repeat between *'s twice having the last knot of **DDHH** 1 inch below last **HB**. There will be 3 sections worked in the same manner.

BRAIDS:

(**NOTE:** Divide **E** so that there are 2 strands to a length). Starting at left and using **B** and **A**, braid a 24 inch length, tie an **OHK** and cut approximately 5 inches from knot. Use **D** with **C**, the 3 **E** lengths, **D** with **C**, and **B** with **A**.

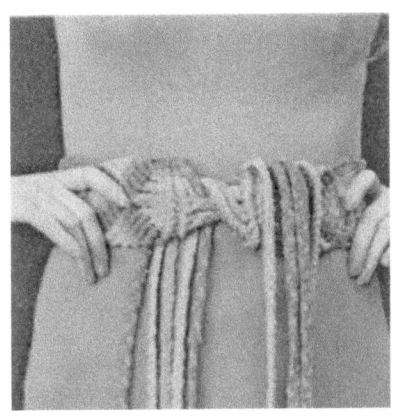

MACRAME DRAWSTRING BAG & BELT
Instruction on page 18

MACRAME BELT

Materials Required:
AMERICAN THREAD

"Aunt Lydia's" Heavy Rug Yarn.

1—70 Yd. Skein each of **A, B, C**, and **D**.

1 Yarn Needle

Measurement: 24 inches.

Suggested Color Scheme: A—Black. **B**—Burnt Orange. **C**—Antique. **D**—White.

Note: All lengths are worked with 2 strands unless otherwise noted.

Cut two 6½ yd lengths and twelve 4 yd lengths of **A**, eight 4 yd lengths each of **B, C** and **D**. The belt will be worked in two halves, each half measuring 12 inches, then sewn together. Take one 6½ yd length of **A**, fold in half, find center and tie an **OHK** 2 inches from either side of center. Secure 4 inch center to board and anchor lengths onto it using **RDHH** in the following sequence: 4 **A** (including the longer length of 4 inch section), 2 **B**, 2 **C**, 4 **D**, 2 **C**, 2 **B**, 4 **A**. Cross center 4 **D** lengths over one another having 2 lengths to the right and 2 to the left. Work each length in **DDHH** leaving lengths used as leaders untied so that the last knot is 1 inch below foundation (first row shaping only). Repeat with each color working half in each direction until **A** lengths remain in the center. Starting on the left, * with **D** tie 8 **VHH**, with **C** tie 7, with **B** tie 3, with **A** tie 2, with **A** tie 3 *. Repeat between *'s in reverse. Using outside **D** length on right, work **HDHH** to left across entire piece and using same length as leader work back to right. With outside **D** on the right work to center in **DDHH** so that last knot is 1 inch below **HB**. Repeat with outside **D** on the left. With these 2 leaders in the center tie 3 **VHH**. Work these leaders in opposite directions forming an X with last knot 1 inch below center of X. With left outside **D** work a **HB** across the entire piece. Using same length as leader work back to the left. Starting on the left * with **D** tie 8 **VHH**, with **C** tie 7, with **B** tie 3, with **A** tie 3, with **A** tie 2 *. Repeat between *'s in reverse. Cross center **A** lengths over each other having four to the left and four to the right. Carry each length to the outside in **DDHH** being sure not to tie any lengths used as leaders, so that last knot is 2 inches below last **HB** worked. Carry all lengths in the same manner until **D** remains in the center. Starting at left * with **A** tie 11 **VHH**, with **A** tie 7, with **B** tie 5, with **C** tie 4 *. Divide the 4 lengths of **D** into 2 lengths having 4 strands each, tie 3 **VHH**. Repeat between *'s in reverse. With left outside **A** work a **HB** across entire piece to the right. Using same length as leader work back to the left. Starting 2 inches below last bar worked, with right outside **A** work a **HB** across entire piece to the left. Using same length as leader work back to the right. With outside 2 **A** lengths on either side tie 8 **VHH**. Divide the center **D** lengths into 4 lengths having 2 strands each. Tie 8 **VHH** with first 2 lengths of **D** and 8 **VHH** with next 2 lengths of **D**. These will be used to form the lacing loops. Sew ends of loops into position. With yarn needle or crochet hook weave in the ends on the back side for at least ½ inch. Trim.

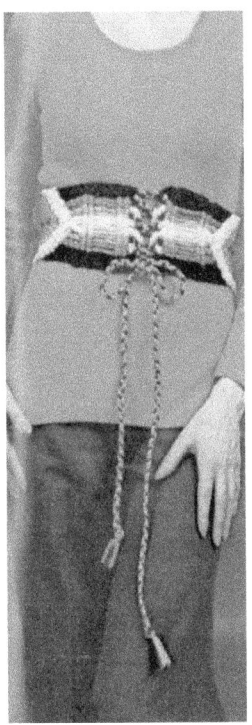

BRAID LACING:

Cut two 2½ yd lengths each of **A**, **C**, and **B**. Tie ends together 2 inches from beginning with an **OHK**. Braid using double strands of color as one. Tie an **OHK** 2 inches from the end. Lace through loops.

MACRAME DRAWSTRING BAG
Size: 12" high, 10" in diameter

Materials Required:

AMERICAN THREAD

"Aunt Lydia's" Heavy Rug Yarn

6—70 Yd. Skeins **A**.

1—70 Yd. Skein each of **B, C, D,** and **E**.

1 Yd. lining fabric

1 Yarn Needle

1 Aluminum Crochet Hook size H or any size hook which will result in stitch gauge below.

Gauge: (For base of bag only):

3 rows = 1 inch, 3 stitches = 1 inch

Measurements:

12 inches high x 10 inches diameter

Color Scheme: **A**—Cream. **B**—Burnt Orange. **C**—Black. **D**—White. **E**—Antique.

Cut 2—13 yd. lengths and 88—3 yd. lengths of **A**, 8—3 yd. lengths each of **B** and **E**, 6—3 yd. lengths of **D** and 16—3 yd. lengths of **C**. Cut a 1 yd. length of **A** for foundation yarn. Tie an **OHK** 2 inches from either end of foundation yarn leaving 32 inches for anchoring lengths. Anchor lengths to foundation using **RDHH**, having **4 RDHH** to an inch, in the following sequence: 1—13 yd. and 5—3 yd. lengths of **A**, 2 **C**, 1 **B**, 1 **E**, 1 **D**, 1 **E**, 1 **B**, 2 **C**, 39 **A**, 4 **C**, 2 **B**, 2 **E**, 4 **D**, 2 **E**, 2 **B**, 4 **C**, 39 **A**, 2 **C**, 1 **B**, 1 **E**, 1 **D**, 1 **E**, 1 **B**, 2 **C**, 5—3 yd. lengths and 1—13 yd. length of **A**.

Note:

There will be four horizontal sections worked in the same pattern. All lengths will be worked with 2 strands of yarn unless otherwise noted.

PATTERN:

** Starting with the first **A** on the left as a leader, work in **HDHH** to the right across the entire piece including the last 13 yd. length. With last length knotted as leader work in **HDHH** to the left across the entire piece. Starting at the left, the first 6 lengths of **A** will be worked to form an angle <. With the 6th **A** in from the left as leader work to the left in **DDHH** having the last knot 1 inch below the last **HB** worked. With the same length as leader work to the right in **DDHH** so that the last knot is 2 inches below last **HB** worked. **NOTE:** Work all angles to correspond with this in size. The next color group will be worked to form a diamond <>. Divide **D** having 1 strand of yarn to a length. These will remain this way throughout work. Work left **D** strand to the left in **DDHH** and back to the center forming an angle <. Work right **D** strand to the right in **DDHH** and back to the center forming an angle >. * The next 6 lengths of **A** will be worked to form an angle >. With the first **A** as a leader work in same manner as the first group of **A** reversing direction. The next 12 lengths of **A** will be worked to form an X. With first length as leader work in **DDHH** to center, knotting each of the next 5 lengths. With last of 12 lengths as leader work to the left, to the center, knotting each of the next 5 lengths. With the 2 leaders knot 3 **VHH** and carry leaders in opposite directions forming the X. Divide the next 3 lengths into 2 lengths of 3 strands each. These will remain this way throughout work. Tie 7 **VHH**. Work the next 12 lengths to form an **X**. Work the next 6 lengths in the same manner as the first group of 6 forming an angle < *. The center color group (next 20 lengths) will be worked to form an X. With first **C** length as leader work in **DDHH** to the center. With first **C** on the right as leader work in **DDHH** to the center. With the center 2 **C** lengths tie 3 **VHH** and carry leaders in opposite directions in **DDHH** forming the X. Repeat between *'s once. Work last color group in same manner as first. Work last **A** group in same manner as first reversing direction to form an angle > **. Repeat between **'s 3 times. * With the left outside length as leader, work a **HB** across entire piece to the right. With last length knotted as leader work a **HB** across entire piece to the left. Repeat from * once. Trim lengths 6 inches below last **HB**.

BASE:

With crochet hook and **A** ch 4, join in first st of ch to form a ring.

1st ROUND: Work 8 sc in ring, join. Do not join or turn unless otherwise indicated.

2nd ROUND: 2 sc in each sc all around (16 sts). Place a marker for each round.

3rd ROUND: * 2 sc in first sc, 1 sc in next sc. Repeat from * all around (24 sts).

4th ROUND: * 1 sc in each of next 3 sc, 2 sc in next sc. Repeat from * all around (30 sts).

5th ROUND: * 1 sc in each of the next 4 sc, 2 sc in next sc. Repeat from * all around (36 sts).

6th ROUND: Repeat 4th Round (45 sts).

7th ROUND: 1 sc in each of the next 2 sc, 2 sc in next sc, * sc in each of the next 4 sc, 2 sc in next sc. Repeat from * to within last 2 sts, 1 sc in each of the last 2 sc (54 sts).

8th ROUND: * 1 sc in each of the next 5 sc, 2 sc in next sc. Repeat from * all around (63 sts).

9th ROUND: 1 sc in each of the next 2 sc, * 2 sc in next sc, sc in each of the next 9 sc, repeat from * to within last st, 2 sc in last sc (70 sts).

10th ROUND: 1 sc in each sc all around (70 sts).

11th ROUND: * 1 sc in each of next 9 sc, 2 sc in next sc. Repeat from * all around (77 sts).

12th ROUND: 1 sc in each sc all around (77 sts).

13th ROUND: * 1 sc in each of the next 6 sc, 2 sc in next sc. Repeat from * all around (88 sts).

14th ROUND: 1 sc in each of the next 2 sc, 2 sc in next sc, * sc in each of the next 4 sc, 2 sc in next sc. Repeat from * all around (106 sts).

15th ROUND: 1 sc in each sc all around, turn.

16th ROUND: Ch 1, 1 sc in each of the first 4 sc; decrease in 5th and 6th sc. (To decrease: Pull up a loop in each of 2 sts, yarn over and work off all loops at one time). * 1 sc in each of the next 8 sc, dec in 9th and 10th sc. Repeat from * all around (95 sts). Join with slip st, cut yarn leaving a 1½ yd. length for sewing.

FINISHING:

Cut pattern for lining using crocheted base and macrame unstitched bag. Sew side seam of bag with an overcast stitch being careful to match patterns. Pin base into position on the lower 2 horizontal bars. Sew with a snug overhand stitch. With right side of bag facing, with crochet hook, and **A**, work 1 sc between each **RDHH** all around the top having 127 sc, join in 1st sc, do not turn.

2nd ROUND: Beading: Ch 3, sc in next sc, * ch 1, skip 1 sc, sc in next sc. Repeat from * all around, join in 2nd st of ch.

3rd ROUND: Ch 4, (counts as 1 dc and 1 ch) * skip 1 sc, dc in ch 1 space, ch 1. Repeat from * all around. Join in 3rd st of ch 4 (64 dc).

4th ROUND: Ch 4, dc in ch 1 space, ch 1, * dc in next ch 1 space, ch 1. Repeat from * all around. Join in 3rd st of ch 4.

5th ROUND: Repeat 4th Round, cut yarn and fasten end under.

HANDLES: (Make 2)

Cut 2—1¾ yd. lengths each of **E**, **B**, and **C**. Tie all lengths together with an **OHK** 1 inch from beginning. Using 2 strands of each color to a length, braid to within 2 inches from end. Tie an **OHK** and trim ends to 1 inch. Weave first braid of handle through beading (3rd Round). Knot ends together with **OHK**. Starting at opposite side, weave 2nd braid through same beading. Knot ends together.

Milton Keynes UK
Ingram Content Group UK Ltd.
UKHW051025250324
439991UK00008B/1039